45 Mercy Street

Anne Sexton

45 Mercy Street

Edited by Linda Gray Sexton

HOUGHTON MIFFLIN COMPANY BOSTON

1976

Some of the poems in this book have appeared in
The Boston Review, Harper's, and *New Republic.*
"June Bug" originally appeared in *The New Yorker* and
"Seagull," "Raccoon," "Seal," "Cow," "Butterfly,"
"Earthworm," "Whale," "Horse," "Swan," "Bat," "Hog,"
"Porcupine," "Hornet," "Star-Nosed Mole," "Snail,"
"Lobster," "Snake," "Moose," "Sheep," "Cockroach,"
and "Coyote" were first published in *Antaeus.*

Library of Congress Cataloging in Publication Data
Sexton, Anne.
    45 Mercy Street.

    I. Title.
PS3537.E915F6   811'.5'4   75–38707
ISBN 0–395–24295–9
ISBN 0–395–24294–0 pbk.

Printed in the United States of America

W   10   9   8   7   6   5   4   3   2   1

For Barbara and the wrecked house
she reconstructs even though it fell
upon her very private beach.

EDITOR'S NOTE

Anne Sexton's voice did not cease with her death. She left two unpublished manuscripts: *45 Mercy Street* and an untitled binder full of new poems. Although she considered the first collection "complete," she was still revising it at the time of her death. In June of 1974, she wrote to her literary agent: "I have actually finished another book, *45 Mercy Street*, but am glad to have the time to reform the poems, rewrite and delete." Ordinarily, Anne Sexton reworked her poems again and again, often changing a line or a word while the "finished" manuscript was in its final stages at the publisher's. Although she was often obdurate — sticking by any aspect of her work that she believed in — she also knew how to use others' criticism to advantage. She relied heavily on her editors, friends, and fellow poets, watching and listening to their reactions. So it began with *45 Mercy Street*, although ultimately she did not find time enough for that final perfection.

45 Mercy Street charts Anne Sexton's poetic growth and the events of her life from 1971 through 1974. The manuscript has been edited but changes are few. All those concerned with the production of the book felt that the basic text must be preserved. As her literary executor, I have altered the placement of a few poems. Having placed them in order in her black binder, she had not yet arrived at a final arrangement, and her trial organization has proved somewhat confusing. The new arrangement allows the poems to build to a clear progression of thought and emotion. The first section has also been re-titled, and I am indebted to Lois Ames for my introduction to the word "hegira."

In preparing 45 *Mercy Street* for press, I have struggled to decipher her handwriting, those crooked black scars which she herself referred to as "a terrible scribble." There are probable alternative readings for a few words, but, apart from these minor uncertainties, the poems themselves have not been edited. Each line appears exactly as she wrote it. Certain poems have been omitted, however, because of their intensely personal content, and the pain their publication would bring to individuals still living. As she commented in February of 1974, "part of 45 *Mercy Street* is still too personal to publish for some time." The complete manuscript, in its original order, has been preserved with all her worksheets, private papers and letters in the Anne Sexton Archive, presently at Boston University.

I thank all those who have supported me during my startling and sometimes painful initiation into "this business of words."

Linda Gray Sexton
September, 1975

CONTENTS

III. The Divorce Papers

IV. Eating the Leftovers

I

Beginning the Hegira

hegira (hĭ-jĭ′rə). noun. A journey or trip especially when undertaken as a means of escaping from an undesirable or dangerous environment; or as a means of arriving at a highly desirable destination.

45 MERCY STREET

In my dream,
drilling into the marrow
of my entire bone,
my real dream,
I'm walking up and down Beacon Hill
searching for a street sign —
namely MERCY STREET.
Not there.

I try the Back Bay.
Not there.
Not there.
And yet I know the number.
45 Mercy Street.
I know the stained-glass window
of the foyer,
the three flights of the house
with its parquet floors.
I know the furniture and
mother, grandmother, great-grandmother,
the servants.
I know the cupboard of Spode,
the boat of ice, solid silver,
where the butter sits in neat squares
like strange giant's teeth
on the big mahogany table.
I know it well.

Not there.

Where did you go?
45 Mercy Street,
with great-grandmother
kneeling in her whale-bone corset
and praying gently but fiercely
to the wash basin,
at five A.M.
at noon
dozing in her wiggy rocker,
grandfather taking a nip in the pantry,
grandmother pushing the bell for the downstairs maid,
and Nana rocking Mother with an oversized flower
on her forehead to cover the curl
of when she was good and when she was . . .
And where she was begat
and in a generation
the third she will beget,
me,
with the stranger's seed blooming
into the flower called *Horrid*.

I walk in a yellow dress
and a white pocketbook stuffed with cigarettes,
enough pills, my wallet, my keys,
and being twenty-eight, or is it forty-five?
I walk. I walk.
I hold matches at the street signs
for it is dark,
as dark as the leathery dead
and I have lost my green Ford,
my house in the suburbs,

two little kids
sucked up like pollen by the bee in me
and a husband
who has wiped off his eyes
in order not to see my inside out
and I am walking and looking
and this is no dream
just my oily life
where the people are alibis
and the street is unfindable for an
entire lifetime.

Pull the shades down —
I don't care!
Bolt the door, mercy,
erase the number,
rip down my street sign,
what can it matter,
what can it matter to this cheapskate
who wants to own the past
that went out on a dead ship
and left me only with paper?

Not there.

I open my pocketbook,
as women do,
and fish swim back and forth
between the dollars and the lipstick.
I pick them out,
one by one
and throw them at the street signs,
and shoot my pocketbook
into the Charles River.

Next I pull the dream off
and slam into the cement wall
of the clumsy calendar
I live in,
my life,
and its hauled up
notebooks.

TALKING TO SHEEP

My life
has appeared unclothed in court,
detail by detail,
death-bone witness by death-bone witness,
and I was shamed at the verdict
and given a cut penny
and the entrails of a cat.
But nevertheless I went on
to the invisible priests,
confessing, confessing
through the wire of hell
and they wet upon me in that phone booth.

Then I accosted winos,
the derelicts of the region,
winning them over into the latrine of my details.
Yes. It was a compulsion
but I denied it, called it fiction
and then the populace screamed *Me too, Me too*
and I swallowed it like my fate.

Now,
in my middle age,
I'm well aware
I keep making statues
of my acts, carving them with my sleep —
or if it is not my life I depict

then someone's close enough to wear my nose —
My nose, my patrician nose,
sniffing at me or following theirs down the street.

Yet even five centuries ago this smelled queer,
confession, confession,
and your devil was thought to push out their eyes
and all the eyes had seen (too much! too much!).
It was proof that you were a needle
to push into their pupils.
And the only cure for such confessions overheard
was to sit in a cold bath for six days,
a bath full of leeches, drawing out your blood
into which confessors had heated the devil in them,
inhabited them with their madness.

It was wise, the wise medical men said,
wise to cry *Baa* and be smiling into your mongoloid hood,
while you simply tended the sheep.
Or else to sew your lips shut
and not let a word or a deadstone sneak out.

I too have my silence,
where I enter another room
and am not only blind,
but speech has flown out of me
and I call it dead
though the respiration be okay.
Perhaps it is a sheep call?
I feel I must learn to speak the *Baa*
of the simple-minded, while my mind
dives into the multi-colored,
crowded voices,

cries for help, *My breasts are off me.*
The transvestite whispering to me,
over and over, *My legs are disappearing.*
My mother, her voice like water,
saying *Fish are cut out of me.*
My father,
his voice thrown into a cigar,
A marble of blood rolls into my heart.
My great aunt,
her voice,
thrown into a lost child at the freaks' circus,
I am the flame swallower
but turn me over in bed
and I am the fat lady.

Yes! While my mind plays simple-minded,
plays dead-woman in neon,
I must recall to say
Baa
to the black sheep I am.

Baa. Baa. Baa.

THE FALLING DOLLS

Dolls,
by the thousands,
are falling out of the sky
and I look up in fear
and wonder who will catch them?
The leaves, holding them like green dishes?
The ponds, open as wine glasses to drink them down?
The tops of buildings to smash in their stomachs
and leave them there to get sooty?
The highways with their hard skins
so that they may be run over like muskrats?
The seas, looking for something to shock the fish?
The electric fences to burn their hair off?
The cornfields where they can lie unpicked?
The national parks where centuries later
they'll be found petrified like stone babies?

I hold open my arms
and catch
one,
two,
three . . . ten in all,
running back and forth like a badminton player,
catching the dolls, the babies I practice upon,
but others crack on the roof
and I dream, awake, I dream of falling dolls

who need cribs and blankets and pajamas
with real feet in them.
Why is there no mother?
Why are all these dolls falling out of the sky?
Was there a father?
Or have the planets cut holes in their nets
and let our childhood out,
or are we the dolls themselves,
born but never fed?

THE MONEY SWING

After "Babylon Revisited" *by F. Scott Fitzgerald*

Mother, Father,
I hold this snapshot of you,
taken, it says, in 1929
on the deck of the yawl.
Mother, Father,
so young, so hot, so jazzy,
so like Zelda and Scott
with drinks and cigarettes and turbans
and designer slacks and frizzy permanents
and all that dough,
what do you say to me now,
here at my sweaty desk in 1971?

I know the ice in your drink is senile.
I know your smile will develop a boil.
You know only that you are on top,
swinging like children on the money swing
up and over, up and over,
until even New York City lies down small.
You know that when winter comes
and the snow comes
that it won't be real snow.
If you don't want it to be snow
you just pay money.

FOOD

I want mother's milk,
that good sour soup.
I want breasts singing like eggplants,
and a mouth above making kisses.
I want nipples like shy strawberries
for I need to suck the sky.
I need to bite also
as in a carrot stick.
I need arms that rock,
two clean clam shells singing *ocean*.
Further I need weeds to eat
for they are the spinach of the soul.
I am hungry and you give me
a dictionary to decipher.
I am a baby all wrapped up in its red howl
and you pour salt into my mouth.
Your nipples are stitched up like sutures
and although I suck
I suck air
and even the big fat sugar moves away.
Tell me! Tell me! Why is it?
I need food
and you walk away reading the paper.

THE CHILD BEARERS

Jean, death comes close to us all,
flapping its awful wings at us
and the gluey wings crawl up our nose.
Our children tremble in their teen-age cribs,
whirling off on a thumb or a motorcycle,
mine pushed into gnawing a stilbestrol cancer
I passed on like hemophilia,
or yours in the seventh grade, with her spleen
smacked in by the balance beam.
And we, mothers, crumpled, and flyspotted
with bringing them this far
can do nothing now but pray.

Let us put your three children
and my two children,
ages ranging from eleven to twenty-one,
and send them in a large air net up to God,
with many stamps, *real* air mail,
and huge signs attached:
SPECIAL HANDLING.
DO NOT STAPLE, FOLD OR MUTILATE!
And perhaps He will notice
and pass a psalm over them
for keeping safe for a whole,
for a whole God-damned life-span.

And not even a muddled angel will
peek down at us in our foxhole.

And He will not have time
to send down an eyedropper of prayer for us,
the mothering thing of us,
as we drop into the soup
and drown
in the worry festering inside us,
lest our children
go so fast
they go.

THE TAKER

While the house was away
and the curtains were baby-sitting,
you made your crossing over.
The pitiless rugs had nothing to say,
the grandfather clock went on with its knitting,
the disposal vomited up chives and clover.
The house became a stage where you played
on the night, my string bean, that you were made.

Our song, *Melancholy Baby*, could not
be heard. *Goodnight Moon* was outgrown,
and two fireflies died unnoticed.
A moth lay down in the jelly pot.
The driveway waited. The grass was mown.
And string bean lay down in her wedding bed.
Her heart went out on a train to meet him
and her mother blessed her,
as best she could,
limb to limb.

THE RISK

When a daughter tries suicide
and the chimney falls down like a drunk
and the dog chews her tail off
and the kitchen blows up its shiny kettle
and the vacuum cleaner swallows its bag
and the toilet washes itself in tears
and the bathroom scales weigh in the ghost
of the grandmother and the windows,
those sky pieces, ride out like boats
and the grass rolls down the driveway
and the mother lies down on her marriage bed
and eats up her heart like two eggs.

PRAYING TO BIG JACK

for Ruthie, my God-child

God, Jack of all trades,
I've got Ruthie's life to trade for today.
She's six. She's got her union card
and a brain tumor, that apple gone sick.
Take in mind, Jack, that her dimple
would erase a daisy. She's one of yours,
small walker of dogs and ice cream.
And she being one of yours
hears the saw lift off her skull
like a baseball cap. Cap off
and then what? The brains as
helpless as oysters in a pint container,
the nerves like phone wires.
God, take care, take infinite care
with the tumor lest it spread like grease.
Ruthie, somewhere in Toledo, has a twin,
mirror girl who plays marbles
and wonders: *Where is the other me?*
The girl of the same dress and my smile?
Today they sing together, they sing for alms.
God have you lapsed?
Are you so bitter with the world
you would put us down the drainpipe at six?

You of the top hat,
Mr. God,
you of the Cross made of lamb bones,

you of the camps, sacking the rejoice out of Germany,
I tell you this . . .
it will not do.
I will run up into the sky and chop wood.
I will run to sea and find a thousand-year servant.
I will run to the cave and bring home a Captain
if you will only, will only,
dear inquisitor.

Banish Ruth, plump Jack,
and you banish all the world.

RED ROSES

Tommy is three and when he's bad
his mother dances with him.
She puts on the record,
"Red Roses for a Blue Lady"
and throws him across the room.
Mind you,
she never laid a hand on him,
only the wall laid a hand on him.
He gets red roses in different places,
the head, that time he was as sleepy as a river,
the back, that time he was a broken scarecrow,
the arm like a diamond had bitten it,
the leg, twisted like a licorice stick,
all the dance they did together,
Blue Lady and Tommy.
You fell, she said, just remember you fell.
I fell, is all he told the doctors
in the big hospital. A nice lady came
and asked him questions but because
he didn't want to be sent away he said, I fell.
He never said anything else although he could talk fine.
He never told about the music
or how she'd sing and shout
holding him up and throwing him.

He pretends he is her ball.
He tries to fold up and bounce

but he squashes like fruit.
For he loves Blue Lady and the spots
of red red roses he gives her.

THE SHOUT

Are you in Eden again, America?
Haggling it out with Adam and his rib?
If so forget them like hamburg!
Look inward, America.
Move our own furniture into the house.
Take little Joe, for instance,
he was as small as a nail
but he shouted the sky down.
The clouds fell down like water-wings.
The stars fell down like slivers of glass.
The trees turned to rubber
and their leaves sat on the ground like shoes.
All the people of America,
those out on the town and
those snugging to their beds,
heard the shout.

A sound like *that*
out of a child's mouth
not to announce the Magi,
not to ward off a beating,
but to show the infernal sleepers
his gift.

They did not know where the sound came from.
Only that it was hungry.

KEEPING THE CITY

"Unless the Lord keepeth the city, the watchman
guardeth in vain."—John F. Kennedy's unspoken words
in Dallas on November 23, 1963.

Once,
in August,
head on your chest,
I heard wings
battering up the place,
something inside trying to fly out
and I was silent
and attentive,
the watchman.
I was your small public,
your small audience
but it was you that was clapping,
it was you untying the snarls and knots,
the webs, all bloody and gluey;
you with your twelve tongues and twelve wings
beating, wresting, beating, beating
your way out of childhood,
that airless net that fastened you down.

Since then I was more silent
though you had gone miles away,
tearing down, rebuilding the fortress.
I was there
but could do nothing
but guard the city
lest it break.

I was silent.
I had a strange idea I could overhear
but that your voice, tongue, wing
belonged solely to you.
The Lord was silent too.
I did not know if he could keep you whole,
where I, miles away, yet head on your chest,
could do nothing. Not a single thing.

The wings of the watchman,
if I spoke, would hurt the bird of your soul
as he nested, bit, sucked, flapped.
I wanted him to fly, burst like a missile from your throat,
burst from the spidery-mother-web,
burst from *Woman* herself
where too many had laid out lights
that stuck to you and left a burn
that smarted into your middle age.

The city
of my choice
that I guard
like a butterfly, useless, useless
in her yellow costume, swirling
swirling around the gates.
The city shifts, falls, rebuilds,
and I can do nothing.
A watchman
should be on the alert,
but never cocksure.
And The Lord —
who knows what he keepeth?

II

Bestiary U.S.A.

(I look at the strangeness in them
and the naturalness they cannot help,
in order to find some virtue in the
beast in me.)

BAT

His awful skin
stretched out by some tradesman
is like my skin, here between my fingers,
a kind of webbing, a kind of frog.
Surely when first born my face was this tiny
and before I was born surely I could fly.
Not well, mind you, only a veil of skin
from my arms to my waist.
I flew at night, too. Not to be seen
for if I were I'd be taken down.
In August perhaps as the trees rose to the stars
I have flown from leaf to leaf in the thick dark.
If you had caught me with your flashlight
you would have seen a pink corpse with wings,
out, out, from her mother's belly, all furry
and hoarse skimming over the houses, the armies.
That's why the dogs of your house sniff me.
They know I'm something to be caught
somewhere in the cemetery hanging upside down
like a misshapen udder.

HOG

Oh you brown bacon machine,
how sweet you lie,
gaining a pound and a half a day,
you rolled-up pair of socks,
you dog's nightmare,
your snout pushed in
but leaking out the ears,
your eyes as soft as eggs,
hog, big as a cannon,
how sweet you lie.

I lie in my bed at night
in the closet of my mind
and count hogs in a pen,
brown, spotted, white, pink, black,
moving on the shuttle toward death
just as my mind moves over
for its own little death.

PORCUPINE

Spine hog,
how do you grow?
Little steel wings
that stick into me.
Knitting needles
that stick into me.
Long steel bullets
that stick into me,
so like the four-inch
screws that hold me
in place, an iron
maiden the doctors
devised.
　　　　Well then,
I'm taking them out,
spine by spine,
somebody else's nails,
not Jesus', not Anne's,
but nails. They
don't belong to the
Brooklyn Bridge,
they don't fit into
the holes of the
White House, they
don't (any longer)
fit into Martin
Luther King, they

won't do in a Kennedy,
they can't make it
with the governors
or the senators,
they push, push,
push into the earth,
bringing forth some
old diamonds we'd never thought of.
And why not, old
Spine Hog U.S.A.?

HORNET

A red-hot needle
hangs out of him, he steers by it
as if it were a rudder, he
would get in the house any way he could
and then he would bounce from window
to ceiling, buzzing and looking for you.
Do not sleep for he is there wrapped in the curtain.
Do not sleep for he is there under the shelf.
Do not sleep for he wants to sew up your skin,
he wants to leap into your body like a hammer
with a nail, do not sleep he wants to get into
your nose and make a transplant, he wants do not
sleep he wants to bury your fur and make
a nest of knives, he wants to slide under your
fingernail and push in a splinter, do not sleep
he wants to climb out of the toilet when you sit on it
and make a home in the embarrassed hair do not sleep
he wants you to walk into him as into a dark fire.

STAR-NOSED MOLE

Mole, angel-dog of the pit,
digging six miles a night,
what's up with you in your sooty suit,
where's your kitchen at?

I find you at the edge of our pond,
drowned, numb drainer of weeds,
insects floating in your belly,
grubs like little fetuses bobbing

and your dear face with its fifth hand,
doesn't it know it's the end of the war?
It's all over, no need to go deep into ponds,
no fires, no cripples left.

                            Mole dog,
I wish your mother would wake you up
and you wouldn't lie there like the Pietà
wearing your cross on your nose.

SNAIL

The snail in his museum
wears his mother all day,
he hides his mysterious bottom
as if it were rotten fruit.
He desires not the kiss.
He desires not the radio.
He desires not directions to Paris.
He desires to lie in his fragile doorway
scratching his back all day.

All this is very well
until hands come like a backhoe
to bring him to the kitchen.
They keep his house.
They swallow the rest.

LOBSTER

A shoe with legs,
a stone dropped from heaven,
he does his mournful work alone,
he is like the old prospector for gold,
with secret dreams of God-heads and fish heads.
Until suddenly a cradle fastens round him
and he is trapped as the U.S.A. sleeps.
Somewhere far off a woman lights a cigarette;
somewhere far off a car goes over a bridge;
somewhere far off a bank is held up.
This is the world the lobster knows not of.
He is the old hunting dog of the sea
who in the morning will rise from it
and be undrowned
and they will take his perfect green body
and paint it red.

SNAKE

Made of old rags of tongues,
of flesh slipped through the abortionist's knife —
you snake thing, made of an army of grapes,
how cleverly you pick your way in and out
of the grass and overhead in the tree.
What can I make of you with my halting footsteps?
Do we go together?
Only by way of Eve's snake
whom I've held up to my man,
time after time, and said,
Let us put him to some use,
let us swallow this snake like a cigar
and allow all our body hair to turn green
with envy.

MOOSE

American Archangel you are going —
your body as big as a moving van —
the houses, the highways are turning you in.
Before my house was, you stood there grazing
and before that my grandfather's home with you
on the wall. Antlers for hat racks
and I felt the rest of your body somewhere outside
the wall merely asking for an invitation.
You stand now in a field in Maine,
hopelessly alive,
your antlers like seaweed,
your face like a wolf's death mask,
your mouth a virgin, your nose a nipple,
your legs muscled up like knitting balls,
your neck mournful as an axe,
and I would like to ask you into my garden
so that I might pack you quickly in salt
and keep your proud body past your mystery
and mine.

SHEEP

Little oily fuzzbear,
wearing your wool full of wood,
Mr. Ba-Ba, you yellow man,
you grease ball of thistles,
you yes sir, yes sir three bags full,
have been the work of the men of my life
for all of my life and the mention of you
turns my hands into green money. No longer.
Now the sheep in Australia and Cape Town
are cheaper and boss the world-wide market.
May they turn sour. May many mean things
happen upon them, no shepherds, no dogs,
a blight of the skin, a mange of the wool,
and they will die eating foreign money,
choking on its green alphabet.

COCKROACH

Roach, foulest of creatures,
who attacks with yellow teeth
and an army of cousins big as shoes,
you are lumps of coal that are mechanized
and when I turn on the light you scuttle
into the corners and there is this hiss upon the land.
Yet I know you are only the common angel
turned into, by way of enchantment, the ugliest.
Your uncle was made into an apple.
Your aunt was made into a Siamese cat,
all the rest were made into butterflies
but because you lied to God outrightly —
told him that all things on earth were in order —
He turned his wrath upon you and said,
I will make you the most loathsome,
I will make you into God's lie,
and never will a little girl fondle you
or hold your dark wings cupped in her palm.

But that was not true. Once in New Orleans
with a group of students a roach fled across
the floor and I shrieked and she picked it up
in her hands and held it from my fear for one hour.
And held it like a diamond ring that should not escape.
These days even the devil is getting overturned
and held up to the light like a glass of water.

RACCOON

Coon, why did you come to this dance
with a mask on? Why not the tin man
and his rainbow girl? Why not Racine,
his hair marcelled down to his chest?
Why not come as a stomach digesting
its worms? Why you little fellow
with your ears at attention and your
nose poking up like a microphone?
You whig emblem, you woman chaser,
why do you dance over the wide lawn tonight
clanging the garbage pail like great silver bells?

SEAL

I dreamt of a seal
with wide wings,
made of vinegar and little boys,
sailing past the star motes,
up over the city of Frisco,
saying forgive me lord
for I have lived so little
I have need of night people.
I have need to see the bum dozing
off on scag, the women in labor
pushing forth a pink head,
lord I need to fly I am sick of
rocks and sea water, I need to
see the moon,
old gyrator,
old butter ball,
and the stars pinching each other
like children.
I want the prairie, the city, the mountain,
I am sick and tired of the rock off Frisco
with its bleating and cowing.
Lord, let me see Jesus before it's all over,
crawling up some mountain, reckless and outrageous,
calling out poems
as he lets out his blood.

EARTHWORM

Slim inquirer, while the old fathers sleep
you are reworking their soil, you have
a grocery store there down under the earth
and it is well stocked with broken wine bottles,
old cigars, old door knobs and earth,
that great brown flour that you kiss each day.
There are dark stars in the cool evening and
you fondle them like killer birds' beaks.
But what I want to know is why when small boys
dig you up for curiosity and cut you in half
why each half lives and crawls away as if whole.
Have you no beginning and end? Which heart is
the real one? Which eye the seer? Why
is it in the infinite plan that you would
be severed and rise from the dead like a gargoyle
with two heads?

WHALE

Whale on the beach, you dinosaur,
what brought you smoothing into this dead harbor?
If you'd stayed inside you could have grown
as big as the Empire State. Still you are not a fish,
perhaps you like the land, you'd had enough of
holding your breath under water. What is it we want
of you? To take our warm blood into the great sea
and prove we are not the sufferers of God?
We are sick of babies crying and the birds flapping
loose in the air. We want the double to be big,
and ominous and we want to remember when you were
money in Massachusetts and yet were wild and rude
and killers. We want our killers dressed in black
like grease for we are sick of writing checks,
putting on our socks and working in the little boxes
we call the office.

HORSE

Horse, you flame thrower,
you shark-mouthed man,
you laughter at the end of poems,
you brown furry locomotive
whipping the snow, I am
a pale shadow beside you.
Your nostrils open like field glasses
and can smell all my fear. I am
a silver spoon. You are a four-footed
wing. If I am thirsty you feed me
through an eyedropper, for you are a
gallon drum. Beside you I feel
like a little girl with a papa
who is screaming.
                              And yet and yet,
field horse lapping the grass
like stars and then your droppings,
sweet melons, all brown and
good for gardens and carrots.
Your soft nose would nuzzle me
and my fear would go out singing
into its own body.

JUNE BUG

June bug came on the first of June,
plucking his guitar at the west window,
telling his whole green story, telling —
little buzzard who is all heart who
wants us to know how expensive it is
to keep the stars in their grainy places,
to keep the moles burning underground,
for the roots are stealing all the water,
and so he pulses at each window, a presence,
a huge hairy question who sees our light
and thinks of it:
                    You are the food,
you are the tooth, you are the husband,
light, light, sieving through the screen
whereon I bounce my big body at you
like shoes after a wedding car.

GULL

You with your wings like spatulas,
letting the blue turn into sugar kisses,
letting the fog slip through your fingertips,
informing the lighthouse like turning on the oven,
sobbing at the fish over the Atlantic,
crying out like young girls in fevers and chills,
crying out like friends who sing from the tavern
of fighting hands, crying out, like a goat with
its mouth full of pearls, snatching the bait
like blood from the coals. Oh Gull of my childhood,
cry over my window over and over, take me back,
oh harbors of oil and cunners, teach me to laugh
and cry again that way that was the good bargain
of youth, when the man following you was not a tail
but an uncle, when the death that came upon you
when you were thirsty was solved by a Coke,
but what can be done gull gull when you turn the sun
on again, a dead fruit
       and all that flies today
is crooked and vain and has been cut from a book.

III

The Divorce Papers

WHERE IT WAS AT BACK THEN

Husband,
last night I dreamt
they cut off your hands and feet.
Husband,
you whispered to me,
Now we are both incomplete.

Husband,
I held all four
in my arms like sons and daughters.
Husband,
I bent slowly down
and washed them in magical waters.

Husband,
I placed each one
where it belonged on you.
"A miracle,"
you said and we laughed
the laugh of the well-to-do.

THE WEDLOCK

My breast waited
shy as a clam
until you came,
Mr. Firecracker,
Mr. Panzer-man.
You with your pogo stick,
you with your bag full of jokes.
At the corner of your eyes,
little incisions,
smile wrinkles that tell and tell.
When I shout *help* in my dream
you do not fold me in like a slipper its foot.

Suppertime I float toward you
from the stewpot
holding poems you shrug off
and you kiss me like a mosquito.
No zing and zap
or ounce of gentleness
and when anger comes
like a finger in a light socket,
you of the karate chop,
you of the Tommy Gun,
force me downwards like a stone.

More often now I am your punching bag.
Most days I'm curled like a spotted dog
at your elbow, Panzer-man.

When I'm crazy a daughter buys
a single yellow rose to come home by.
Home is our spy pond pool in the backyard,
the willow with its spooky yellow fingers
and the great orange bed where we lie
like two frozen paintings in a field of poppies.

LANDSCAPE WINTER

Snow, out over the elephant's rump,
my rock outside my word-window,
where it lies in a doze on the front lawn.
Oak leaves, each separate and pink
in the setting sun, as good cows' tongues.
The snow far off on the pine
nesting into the needles
like addicts into their fix.
The mailbox as stiff as a soldier
but wearing a chef's hat.
The ground is full.
It will not eat any more.
Armies of angels have sunk onto it
with their soft parachutes.

And within the house
ashes are being stuffed into my marriage,
fury is lapping the walls,
dishes crack on the shelves,
a strangler needs my throat,
the daughter has ceased to eat anything,
the wife speaks of this
but only the ice cubes listen.

The sweat of fear pumps inside me.
In my sleep I wet the bed,
the marriage bed,

three nights in a row
and soon, soon I'd better run out
while there is time.

Yet, right now,
the outside world seems oblivious
and the snow is happy and all is quiet
as the night waits for its breakfast.

DESPAIR

Who is he?
A railroad track toward hell?
Breaking like a stick of furniture?
The hope that suddenly overflows the cesspool?
The love that goes down the drain like spit?
The love that said *forever, forever*
and then runs you over like a truck?
Are you a prayer that floats into a radio advertisement?
Despair,
I don't like you very well.
You don't suit my clothes or my cigarettes.
Why do you locate here
as large as a tank,
aiming at one half of a lifetime?
Couldn't you just go float into a tree
instead of locating here at my roots,
forcing me out of the life I've led
when it's been my belly so long?

All right!
I'll take you along on the trip
where for so many years
my arms have been speechless.

DIVORCE

I have killed our lives together,
axed off each head,
with their poor blue eyes stuck in a beach ball
rolling separately down the drive.
I have killed all the good things,
but they are too stubborn for me.
They hang on.
The little words of companionship
have crawled into their graves,
the thread of compassion,
dear as a strawberry,
the mingling of bodies
that bore two daughters within us,
the look of you dressing,
early,
all the separate clothes, neat and folded,
you sitting on the edge of the bed
polishing your shoes with boot black,
and I loved you then, so wise from the shower,
and I loved you many other times
and I have been, for months,
trying to drown it,
to push it under,
to keep its great red tongue
under like a fish,
but wherever I look they are on fire,
the bass, the bluefish, the wall-eyed flounder

blazing among the kelp and seaweed
like many suns battering up the waves
and my love stays bitterly glowing,
spasms of it will not sleep,
and I am helpless and thirsty and need shade
but there is no one to cover me —
not even God.

WAKING ALONE

Skull,
museum object,
I could squash you like a rotten melon,
but I would rather — no, I need
to hold you gently like a puppy,
to give you milk and berries for your dear mouth,
husband, husband.
I lust for your smile,
spread open like an old flower,
and your eyes, blue moons,
and your chin, ever Nazi, ever stubborn,
and what can I do with this memory?
Shake the bones out of it?
Defoliate the smile?
Stub out the chin with cigarettes?
Take the face of the man I love
and squeeze my foot into it
when all the while my heart is making a museum?
I love you the way the oboe plays.
I love you the way skinny dipping makes my body feel.
I love you the way a ripe artichoke tastes.
Yet I fear you,
as one in the desert fears the sun.
True.
True.
Yet love enters my blood like an I.V.,
dripping in its little white moments.

In drips the whiplash you delivered,
the Thomas collar I wore,
and then in comes you, ordering wine,
fixing my beach umbrella, mowing grass,
making my kitchen happy with a charcoal steak,
and I come back again to your skull,
the ruffly hair of the morning
that I wasn't allowed to touch,
and then I come back to you saying,
(as I was saying the truth)
my ears are turned off.
And I don't know,
don't know,
if we belong together or apart,
except that my soul lingers over the skin of you
and I wonder if I'm ruining all we had,
and had not,
by making this break,
this torn wedding ring,
this wrenched life
this God who is only half a God,
having separated the resurrection
from the glory,
having ripped the cross off Jesus
and left only the nails.
Husband,
Husband,
I hold up my hand and see
only nails.

BAYONET

What can I do with this bayonet?
Make a rose bush of it?
Poke it into the moon?
Shave my legs with its sliver?
Spear a goldfish?
No. No.

It was made
in my dream
for you.
My eyes were closed.
I was curled fetally
and yet I held a bayonet
that was for the earth of your stomach.
The belly button singing its puzzle.
The intestines winding like the alpine roads.
It was made to enter you
as you have entered me
and to cut the daylight into you
and let out your buried heartland,
to let out the spoon you have fed me with,
to let out the bird that said *fuck you,*
to carve him onto a sculpture until he is white
and I could put him on a shelf,
an object unthinking as a stone,
but with all the vibrations
of a crucifix.

THE WEDDING RING DANCE

I dance in circles holding
the moth of the marriage,
thin, sticky, fluttering
its skirts, its webs.
The moth oozing a tear,
or is it a drop of urine?
The moth, grinning like a pear,
or is it teeth
clamping the iron maiden shut?

The moth,
who is my mother,
who is my father,
who was my lover,
floats airily out of my hands
and I dance slower,
pulling off the fat diamond engagement ring,
pulling off the elopement wedding ring,
and holding them, clicking them
in thumb and forefinger,
the indent of twenty-five years,
like a tiny rip leaving its mark,
the tiny rip of a tiny earthquake.
Underneath the soil lies the violence,
the shift, the crack of continents,
the anger,

and above only a cut,
a half-inch space to stick a pencil in.

The finger is scared
but it keeps its long numb place.
And I keep dancing,
a sort of waltz,
clicking the two rings,
all of a life at its last cough,
as I swim through the air of the kitchen,
and the same radio plays its songs
and I make a small path through them
with my bare finger and my funny feet,
doing the undoing dance,
on April 14th, 1973,
letting my history rip itself off me
and stepping into
something unknown
and transparent,
but all ten fingers stretched outward,
flesh extended as metal
waiting for a magnet.

WHEN THE GLASS OF MY BODY BROKE

Oh mother of sex,
lady of the staggering cuddle,
where do these hands come from?
A man, a Moby Dick of a man,
a swimmer going up and down in his brain,
the gentleness of wine in his fingertips,
where do these hands come from?
I was born a glass baby and nobody picked me up
except to wash the dust off me.
He has picked me up and licked me alive.

Hands
growing like ivy over me,
hands growing out of me like hair,
yet turning into fire grass,
planting an iris in my mouth,
spinning and blue,
the nipples turning into wings,
the lips turning into days that would not give birth,
days that would not hold us in their house,
days that would not wrap us in their secret lap,
and yet hands, hands growing out of pictures,
hands crawling out of the walls,
hands that excite oblivion,
like a wind,
a strange wind
from somewhere tropic

making a storm between my blind legs,
letting me lift the mask of the child from my face,
while all the toy villages fall
and I sink softly into
the heartland.

THE BREAK AWAY

Your daisies have come
on the day of my divorce:
the courtroom a cement box,
a gas chamber for the infectious Jew in me
and a perhaps land, a possibly promised land
for the Jew in me,
but still a betrayal room for the till-death-do-us —
and yet a death, as in the unlocking of scissors
that makes the now separate parts useless,
even to cut each other up as we did yearly
under the crayoned-in sun.
The courtroom keeps squashing our lives as they break
into two cans ready for recycling,
flattened tin humans
and a tin law,
even for my twenty-five years of hanging on
by my teeth as I once saw at Ringling Brothers.
The gray room:
Judge, lawyer, witness
and me and invisible Skeezix,
and all the other torn
enduring the bewilderments
of their division.

Your daisies have come
on the day of my divorce.
They arrive like round yellow fish,

sucking with love at the coral of our love.
Yet they wait,
in their short time,
like little utero half-borns,
half killed, thin and bone soft.
They know they are about to die,
but breathe like premies, in and out,
upon my kitchen table.
They breathe the air that stands
for twenty-five illicit days,
the sun crawling inside the sheets,
the moon spinning like a tornado
in the washbowl,
and we orchestrated them both,
calling ourselves TWO CAMP DIRECTORS.
There was a song, our song on your cassette,
that played over and over
and baptised the prodigals.
It spoke the unspeakable,
as the rain will on an attic roof,
letting the animal join its soul
as we kneeled before a miracle —
forgetting its knife.

The daisies confer
in the old-married kitchen
papered with blue and green chefs
who call out *pies, cookies, yummy,*
at the charcoal and cigarette smoke
they wear like a yellowy salve.
The daisies absorb it all —
the twenty-five-year-old sanctioned love
(If one could call such handfuls of fists

and immobile arms *that!*)
and on this day my world rips itself up
while the country unfastens along
with its perjuring king and his court.
It unfastens into an abortion of belief,
as in me —
the legal rift —
as one *might* do with the daisies
but does not
for they stand for a love
undergoing open heart surgery
that might take
if one prayed tough enough.
And yet I demand,
even in prayer,
that I am not a thief,
a mugger of need,
and that your heart survive
on its own,
belonging only to itself,
whole, entirely whole,
and workable
in its dark cavern under your ribs.

I pray it will know truth,
if truth catches in its cup
and yet I pray, as a child would,
that the surgery take.

I dream it is taking.
Next I dream the love is swallowing itself.
Next I dream the love is made of glass,
glass coming through the telephone

that is breaking slowly,
day by day, into my ear.
Next I dream that I put on the love
like a lifejacket and we float,
jacket and I,
we bounce on that priest-blue.
We are as light as a cat's ear
and it is safe,
safe far too long!
And I awaken quickly and go to the opposite window
and peer down at the moon in the pond
and know that beauty has walked over my head,
into this bedroom and out,
flowing out through the window screen,
dropping deep into the water
to hide.

I will observe the daisies
fade and dry up
until they become flour,
snowing themselves onto the table
beside the drone of the refrigerator,
beside the radio playing Frankie
(as often as FM will allow)
snowing lightly, a tremor sinking from the ceiling —
as twenty-five years split from my side
like a growth that I sliced off like a melanoma.

It is six P.M. as I water these tiny weeds
and their little half-life,
their numbered days
that raged like a secret radio,

recalling love that I picked up innocently,
yet guiltily,
as my five-year-old daughter
picked gum off the sidewalk
and it became suddenly an elastic miracle.

For me it was love found
like a diamond
where carrots grow —
the glint of diamond on a plane wing,
meaning: DANGER! THICK ICE!
but the good crunch of that orange,
the diamond, the carrot,
both with four million years of resurrecting dirt,
and the love,
although Adam did not know the word,
the love of Adam
obeying his sudden gift.

You, who sought me for nine years,
in stories made up in front of your naked mirror
or walking through rooms of fog women,
you trying to forget the mother
who built guilt with the lumber of a locked door
as she sobbed her soured milk and fed you loss
through the keyhole,
you who wrote out your own birth
and built it with your own poems,
your own lumber, your own keyhole,
into the trunk and leaves of your manhood,
you, who fell into my words, years
before you fell into me (the other,
both the Camp Director and the camper),

you who baited your hook with wide-awake dreams,
and calls and letters and once a luncheon,
and twice a reading by me for you.
But I wouldn't!

Yet this year,
yanking off all past years,
I took the bait
and was pulled upward, upward,
into the sky and was held by the sun —
the quick wonder of its yellow lap —
and became a woman who learned her own skin
and dug into her soul and found it full,
and you became a man who learned his own skin
and dug into his manhood, his humanhood
and found you were as real as a baker
or a seer
and we became a home,
up into the elbows of each other's soul,
without knowing —
an invisible purchase —
that inhabits our house forever.

We were
blessed by the House-Dic
by the altar of the color T.V.
and somehow managed to make a tiny marriage,
a tiny marriage
called belief,
as in the child's belief in the tooth fairy,
so close to absolute,
so daft within a year or two.

The daisies have come
for the last time.
And I who have,
each year of my life,
spoken to the tooth fairy,
believing in her,
even when I *was* her,
am helpless to stop your daisies from dying,
although your voice cries into the telephone:
Marry me! Marry me!
and my voice speaks onto these keys tonight:
The love is in dark trouble!
The love is starting to die,
right now —
we are in the process of it.
The empty process of it.

I see two deaths,
and the two men plod toward the mortuary of my heart,
and though I willed one away in court today
and I whisper dreams and birthdays into the other,
they both die like waves breaking over me
and I am drowning a little,
but always swimming
among the pillows and stones of the breakwater.
And though your daisies are an unwanted death,
I wade through the smell of their cancer
and recognize the prognosis,
its cartful of loss . . .

I say now,
you gave what you could.

It was quite a ferris wheel to spin on!
and the dead city of my marriage
seems less important
than the fact that the daisies came weekly,
over and over,
likes kisses that can't stop themselves.

There sit two deaths on November 5th, 1973.
Let one be forgotten —
Bury it! Wall it up!
But let me not forget the man
of my child-like flowers
though he sinks into the fog of Lake Superior,
he remains, his fingers the marvel
of fourth of July sparklers,
his furious ice cream cones of licking,
remains to cool my forehead with a washcloth
when I sweat into the bathtub of his being.

For the rest that is left:
name it gentle,
as gentle as radishes inhabiting
their short life in the earth,
name it gentle,
gentle as old friends waving *so long* at the window,
or in the drive,
name it gentle as maple wings singing
themselves upon the pond outside,
as sensuous as the mother-yellow in the pond,
that night that it was ours,
when our bodies floated and bumped
in moon water and the cicadas
called out like tongues.

Let such as this
be resurrected in all men
wherever they mold their days and nights
as when for twenty-five days and nights you molded mine
and planted the seed that dives into my God
and will do so forever
no matter how often I sweep the floor.

THE STAND-INS

In the dream
the swastika is neon
and flashes like a strobe light
into my eyes, all colors,
all vibrations
and I see the killer in him
and he turns on an oven,
an oven, an oven, an oven
and on a pie plate he sticks
in my Yellow Star
and then
then when it is ready for serving —
this dream goes off into the wings
and on stage The Cross appears,
with Jesus sticking to it
and He is breathing
and breathing
and He is breathing
and breathing
and then He speaks,
a kind of whisper,
and says . . .
This is the start.
This is the end.
This is a light.
This is a start.

I woke.
I did not know the hour,
an hour of night like thick scum
but I considered the dreams,
the two: Swastika, Crucifix,
and said: Oh well,
it doesn't belong to me,
if a cigar can be a cigar
then a dream can be a dream.
Right?
Right?
And went back to sleep
and another start.

THE LOVE PLANT

A freak but moist flower
tangles my lungs, knits into my heart,
crawls up my throat
and sucks like octopi on my tongue.
You planted it happily last summer
and I let it take root with my moon-hope,
not knowing it would come to crowd me out,
to explode inside me this March.
All winter trying to diminish it,
I felt it enlarge.
But of course never spoke to you of this,
for my sanity was awful enough,
and I felt compelled to think only of yours.
Now that you have gone for always
why does not the plant shrivel up?
I try to force it away.
I swallow stones.
Three times I swallow slender vials
with crossbones on them.
But it thrives on their liquid solution.
I light matches and put them in my mouth,
and my teeth melt but the greenery hisses on.
I drink blood from my wrists
and the green slips out like a bracelet.
Couldn't one of my keepers get a lawn mower
and chop it down if I turned inside out for an hour?
This flower, this pulp, the hay stuff

has got me, got me.
Apparently both of us are unkillable.

I am coughing. I am gagging. I feel it enter
the nasal passages, the sinus, lower, upper
and thus to the brain — spurting out of my eyes,
I must find a surgeon who will cut it out, burn it out
as they do sometimes with violent epileptics.
I will dial one quickly before I erupt!

Would you guess at it
if you looked at me swinging down Comm. Ave.
in my long black coat with its fur hood,
and my long pink skirt poking out step by step?
That under the coat, the pink, the bra, the pants,
in the recesses where love knelt
a coughing plant is smothering me?

Perhaps I am becoming unhuman
and should accept its natural order?
Perhaps I am becoming part of the green world
and maybe a rose will just pop out of my mouth?
Oh passerby, let me bite it off and spit it at you
so you can say "How nice!" and nod your thanks
and walk three blocks to your lady love
and she will stick it behind her ear
not knowing it will crawl into her ear, her brain
and drive her mad.

Then she will be like me —
a pink doll with her frantic green stuffing.

KILLING THE LOVE

I am the love killer,
I am murdering the music we thought so special,
that blazed between us, over and over.
I am murdering me, where I kneeled at your kiss.
I am pushing knives through the hands
that created two into one.
Our hands do not bleed at this,
they lie still in their dishonor.
I am taking the boats of our beds
and swamping them, letting them cough on the sea
and choke on it and go down into nothing.
I am stuffing your mouth with your
promises and watching
you vomit them out upon my face.
The Camp we directed?
I have gassed the campers.

Now I am alone with the dead,
flying off bridges,
hurling myself like a beer can into the wastebasket.
I am flying like a single red rose,
leaving a jet stream
of solitude
and yet I feel nothing,
though I fly and hurl,
my insides are empty
and my face is as blank as a wall.

Shall I call the funeral director?
He could put our two bodies into one pink casket,
those bodies from before,
and someone might send flowers,
and someone might come to mourn
and it would be in the obits,
and people would know that something died,
is no more, speaks no more, won't even
drive a car again and all of that.

When a life is over,
the one you were living for,
where do you go?

I'll work nights.
I'll dance in the city.
I'll wear red for a burning.
I'll look at the Charles very carefully,
wearing its long legs of neon.
And the cars will go by.
The cars will go by.
And there'll be no scream
from the lady in the red dress
dancing on her own Ellis Island,
who turns in circles,
dancing alone
as the cars go by.

THE RED DANCE

There was a girl
who danced in the city that night,
that April 22nd,
all along the Charles River.
It was as if one hundred men were watching
or do I mean the one hundred eyes of God?
The yellow patches in the sycamores
glowed like miniature flashlights.
The shadows, the skin of them
were ice cubes that flashed
from the red dress to the roof.
Mile by mile along the Charles she danced
past the benches of lovers,
past the dogs pissing on the benches.
She had on a red, red dress
and there was a small rain
and she lifted her face to it
and thought it part of the river.
And cars and trucks went by
on Memorial Drive.
And the Harvard students in the brick
hallowed houses studied Sappho in cement rooms.
And this Sappho danced on the grass
and danced and danced and danced.
It was a death dance.
The Larz Anderson bridge wore its lights
and many cars went by,

and a few students strolling under
their Coop umbrellas.
And a black man who asked this Sappho the time,
the time, as if her watch spoke.
Words were turning into grease,
and she said, "Why do you lie to me?"
And the waters of the Charles were beautiful,
sticking out in many colored tongues
and this strange Sappho knew she would enter the lights
and be lit by them and sink into them.
And how the end would come —
it had been foretold to her —
she would aspirate swallowing a fish,
going down with God's first creature
dancing all the way.

THE INVENTORY OF GOODBYE

I have a pack of letters.
I have a pack of memories.
I could cut out the eyes of both.
I could wear them like a patchwork apron.
I could stick them in the washer, the drier,
and maybe some of the pain would float off like dirt?
Perhaps down the disposal I could grind up the loss.
Besides — what a bargain — no expensive phone calls.
No lengthy trips on planes in the fog.
No manicky laughter or blessings from an odd-lot priest.
That priest is probably still floating on a fog pillow.
Blessing us. Blessing us.

Am I to bless the lost you,
sitting here with my clumsy soul?
Propaganda time is over.
I sit here on the spike of truth.
No one to hate except the slim fish of memory
that slides in and out of my brain.
No one to hate except the acute feel of my nightgown
brushing my body like a light that has gone out.
It recalls the kiss we invented, tongues like poems,
meeting, returning, inviting, causing a fever of need.
Laughter, maps, cassettes, touch singing its path —
all to be broken and laid away in a tight strongbox.
The monotonous dead clog me up and there is only
black done in black that oozes from the strongbox.

I must disembowel it and then set the heart, the legs,
of two who were one upon a large woodpile
and ignite, as I was once ignited, and let it whirl
into flame, reaching the sky
making it dangerous with its red.

THE LOST LIE

There is rust in my mouth,
the stain of an old kiss.
And my eyes are turning purple,
my mouth is glue
and my hands are two stones
and the heart,
is still there,
that place where love dwelt
but it is nailed into place.
Still I feel no pity for these oddities,
in fact the feeling is one of hatred.
For it is only the child in me bursting out
and I keep plotting how to kill her.

Once there was a woman,
full as a theater of moon
and love begot love
and the child, when she peeked out,
did not hate herself back then.
Funny, funny, love what you do.
But today I roam a dead house,
a frozen kitchen, a bedroom
like a gas chamber.
The bed itself is an operating table
where my dreams slice me into pieces.

Oh love,
the terror,

the fright wig,
that your dear curly head
was, was, was, was.

END, MIDDLE, BEGINNING

There was an unwanted child.
Aborted by three modern methods
she hung on to the womb,
hooked onto it
building her house into it
and it was to no avail,
to black her out.

At her birth
she did not cry,
spanked indeed,
but did not yell —
instead snow fell out of her mouth.

As she grew, year by year,
her hair turned like a rose in a vase,
and bled down her face.
Rocks were placed on her to keep
the growing silent,
and though they bruised,
they did not kill,
though kill was tangled into her beginning.

They locked her in a football
but she merely curled up
and pretended it was a warm doll's house.
They pushed insects in to bite her off

and she let them crawl into her eyes
pretending they were a puppet show.

Later, later,
grown fully, as they say,
they gave her a ring,
and she wore it like a root
and said to herself,
"To be not loved is the human condition,"
and lay like a statue in her bed.

Then once,
by terrible chance,
love took her in his big boat
and she shoveled the ocean
in a scalding joy.

Then,
slowly,
love seeped away,
the boat turned into paper
and she knew her fate,
at last.
Turn where you belong,
into a deaf mute
that metal house,
let him drill you into no one.

IV

Eating the Leftovers

CIGARETTES AND WHISKEY
AND WILD, WILD WOMEN

(from a song)

Perhaps I was born kneeling,
born coughing on the long winter,
born expecting the kiss of mercy,
born with a passion for quickness
and yet, as things progressed,
I learned early about the stockade
or taken out, the fume of the enema.
By two or three I learned not to kneel,
not to expect, to plant my fires underground
where none but the dolls, perfect and awful,
could be whispered to or laid down to die.

Now that I have written many words,
and let out so many loves, for so many,
and been altogether what I always was —
a woman of excess, of zeal and greed,
I find the effort useless.
Do I not look in the mirror,
these days,
and see a drunken rat avert her eyes?
Do I not feel the hunger so acutely
that I would rather die than look
into its face?
I kneel once more,
in case mercy should come
in the nick of time.

THE PASSION OF THE MAD RABBIT

While the carrots sang arias into the holy earth
and the snowmen turned into bronze weathervanes,
I underwent a removal, tearing my skin off me,
plucking out the eyes like Ping-Pong balls,
squashing the shriek of my heart like a phone off the hook —
and as these phenomena occurred, a fool walked straight into
    me.
He was named Mr. Rabbit. My own voice spoke to people,
anyone, friends, strangers on the street, saying,
"I am Mr. Rabbit." The flesh itself had become mad
and at three mirrors this was confirmed.

Next it was bad Friday and they nailed me up
like a scarecrow and many gathered eating popcorn, carrying
hymnals or balloons. There were three of us there,
though *they* appeared normal. My ears, so pink like powder,
were nailed. My paws, sweet as baby mittens, were nailed.
And my two fuzzy ankles. I said, "Pay no attention. I am
    crazy."
But some giggled and some knelt. My oxygen became tiny
and blood rang over and over in my head like a bell.
The others died, the luck of it blurting through them.
I could not. I was a silly broken umbrella
and oblivion would not kiss me. For three days it
was thus.

Then they took me down and had a conference.
It is Easter, they said, and you are the Easter Bunny.

Then they built a great pyre of kindling and laid me on top
and just before the match they handed me a pink basket
of eggs the color of the circus.
Fire lit, I tossed the eggs to them, *Hallelujah* I sang
    to the eggs,
singing as I burned to nothing in the tremor of the flames.
My blood came to a boil as I looked down the throat of
    madness,
but singing yellow egg, blue egg, pink egg, red egg, green
    egg,
Hallelujah, to each hard-boiled-colored egg.

In place of the Lord,
I whispered,
a fool has risen.

THE ANGEL FOOD DOGS

Leaping, leaping, leaping,
down, line by line,
growling at the cadavers,
filling the holy jugs with their piss,
falling into windows and mauling the parents,
but soft, kiss-soft,
and sobbing sobbing
into their awful dog dish.

No point? No twist for you
in my white tunnel?
Let me speak plainly,
let me whisper it from the podium —

Mother, may I use you as a pseudonym?
May I take the dove named Mary
and shove out Anne?
May I take my check book, my holographs,
my eight naked books,
and sign it Mary, Mary, Mary
full of grace?
I know my name is not offensive
but my feet hang in the noose.
I want to be white.
I want to be blue.
I want to be a bee digging into an onion heart,
as you did to me, dug and squatted
long after death and its fang.

Hail Mary, full of me,
Nibbling in the sitting room of my head.
Mary, Mary, virgin forever,
whore forever,
give me your name,
give me your mirror.
Boils fester in my soul,
so give me your name so I may kiss them,
and they will fly off,
nameless
but named,
and they will fly off like angel food dogs
with thee
and with thy spirit.
Let me climb the face of my kitchen dog
and fly off into my terrified years.

LEAVES THAT TALK

Yes.
It's May 20th and the leaves,
green, green, wearing their masks
and speaking, calling out their Sapphic loves,
are here — here — here —
calling out their death wish:

"Anne, Anne, come to us."

to die of course. Come when listening
to the voices of the doves
that burst in them and out of them.
I mean their veins, their hearts
who scare you and beguile you
with their woman apron lives,
their doves' arms flapping
from their cage, their brown stick branches.

I told someone once how they called to me,
sang to me, and that someone fled.
Now I will tell a priest
or is it a priestess?
Both, one and all and the same.
They call, though I sit here
sensibly behind my window screen.
They call, even if I'm pinned behind bars.
They call, they call their green death call.

They want me. They need me.
I belong lying down under them,
letting the green coffin fold and unfold
above me as I go out.

I flee. I flee.
I block my ears and eat salami.
I turn on THE song of THE LADY
but the leaves' song crawls through
and into it and mixes like a dream in a dream.
I confess. I confess.
They steam all summer,
calling dark and light and moonstone
and they do not shut up.
They do not.

It is bad for me, dear confessor,
and yet I am in love with it.
It has a body.
It has many bodies.
I do not believe in ghosts
(very much)
but I wonder if they aren't my whole past —
the generation of women, down the line,
the genealogical line right to the *Mayflower*,
and William Brewster and his woman
who rolled herself sick unto death
until she reached this promised land.
Oh well — whoever my green girls are —
they *are*.

I dream it's the fourth of July
and I'm having a love affair

with grandfather (his real birthday)
and that the leaves fall off,
clank, clank,
crashing down like stones, New England
stones, one by one,
and in my dream
grandfather touches my neck and breast
and says, "Do not be afraid!
It's only the leaves falling!"
There are one hundred thousand woman cries,
tree by tree, and I scream out in my fear
that my green ladies are leaving,
my lovely obsessions,
and I need them.
I sob.
I wake up.
Kleenex.
Grandfather.

And, dear God,
I am Rip van Winkle.
It is six A.M.
July 5th, 1974,
and the branches are bare.
The leaves lie in green mounds,
like fake green snow huts.
And from the window as I peer out,
I see they have left their cages forever —
those wiry, spidery branches —
for me to people
someday soon when I turn green
and faithless to the summer.

"DADDY" WARBUCKS

In Memoriam

What's missing is the eyeballs
in each of us, but it doesn't matter
because you've got the bucks, the bucks, the bucks.
You let me touch them, fondle the green faces
lick at their numbers and it lets you be
my "Daddy!" "Daddy!" and though I fought all alone
with molesters and crooks, I knew your money
would save me, your courage, your "I've had
considerable experience as a soldier . . .
fighting to win millions for myself, it's true.
But I *did* win," and me praying for "our men out there"
just made it okay to be an orphan whose blood was no one's,
whose curls were hung up on a wire machine and electrified,
while you built and unbuilt intrigues called nations,
and did in the bad ones, always, always,
and always came at my perils, the black Christs of childhood,
always came when my heart stood naked in the street
and they threw apples at it or twelve-day-old-dead-fish.

"Daddy!" "Daddy," we all won that war,
when you sang me the money songs
Annie, Annie you sang
and I knew you drove a pure gold car
and put diamonds in your coke
for the crunchy sound, the adorable sound
and the moon too was in your portfolio,
as well as the ocean with its sleepy dead.

And I was always brave, wasn't I?
I never bled?
I never saw a man expose himself.
No. No.
I never saw a drunkard in his blubber.
I never let lightning go in one ear and out the other.
And all the men out there were never to come.
Never, like a deluge, to swim over my breasts
and lay their lamps in my insides.
No. No.
Just me and my "Daddy"
and his tempestuous bucks
rolling in them like corn flakes
and only the bad ones died.

But I died yesterday,
"Daddy," I died,
swallowing the Nazi-Jap-animal
and it won't get out
it keeps knocking at my eyes,
my big orphan eyes,
kicking! Until eyeballs pop out
and even my dog puts up his four feet
and lets go
of his military secret
with his big red tongue
flying up and down
like yours should have

as we board our velvet train.

DIVORCE, THY NAME IS WOMAN

I am divorcing daddy — Dybbuk! Dybbuk!
I have been doing it daily all my life
since his sperm left him
drilling upwards and stuck to an egg.
Fetus, fetus — glows and glows in that home
and bursts out, electric, demanding moths.

For years it was woman to woman,
breast, crib, toilet, dolls, dress-ups.
WOMAN! WOMAN!
Daddy of the whiskies, daddy of the rooster breath,
would visit and then dash away
as if I were a disease.

Later,
when blood and eggs and breasts
dropped onto me,
Daddy and his whiskey breath
made a long midnight visit
in a dream that is not a dream
and then called his lawyer quickly.
Daddy divorcing me.

I have been divorcing him ever since,
going into court with Mother as my witness
and both long dead or not
I am still divorcing him,

adding up the crimes
of how he came to me,
how he left me.

I am pacing the bedroom.
Opening and shutting the windows.
Making the bed and pulling it apart.
I am tearing the feathers out of the pillows,
waiting, waiting for Daddy to come home
and stuff me so full of our infected child
that I turn invisible, but married,
at last.

THE FIERCENESS OF FEMALE

I am spinning,
I am spinning on the lips,
they remove my shadow,
my phantom from my past,
they invented a timetable of tongues,
that take up all my attention.
Wherein there is no room.
No bed.
The clock does not tick
except where it vibrates my 4000 pulses,
and where all was absent,
all is two,
touching like a choir of butterflies,
and like the ocean,
pushing toward land
and receding
and pushing
with a need that gallops
all over my skin,
yelling at the reefs.

I unknit.
Words fly out of place
and I, long into the desert,
drink and drink
and bow my head to that meadow
the breast, the melon in it,

and then the intoxicating flower of it.
Our hands that stroke each other
the nipples like baby starfish —
to make our lips sucking into lunatic rings
until they are bubbles,
our fingers naked as petals
and the world pulses on a swing.
I raise my pelvis to God
so that it may know the truth of how
flowers smash through the long winter.

THE BIG BOOTS OF PAIN

There can be certain potions
needled in by the clock
for the body's fall from grace,
to untorture and to plead for.
These I have known
and would sell all my furniture
and books and assorted goods
to avoid, and more, more.

But the other pain . . .
I would sell my life to avoid
the pain that begins in the crib
with its bars or perhaps
with your first breath
when the planets drill
your future into you
for better or worse
as you marry life
and the love that gets doled out
or doesn't.

I find now, swallowing one teaspoon
of pain, that it drops downward
to the past where it mixes
with last year's cupful
and downward into a decade's quart
and downward into a lifetime's ocean.

I alternate treading water
and deadman's float.

The teaspoon ought to be bearable
if it didn't mix into the reruns
and thus enlarge into what it is not,
a sea pest's sting turning promptly
into the shark's neat biting off
of a leg because the soul
wears a magnifying glass.
Kicking the heart
with pain's big boots running up and down
the intestines like a motorcycle racer.

Yet one does get out of bed
and start over, plunge into the day
and put on a hopeful look
and does not allow fear to build a wall
between you and an old friend
or a new friend and reach out your hand,
shutting down the thought that
an axe may cut it off unexpectedly.
One learns not to blab about all this
except to yourself or the typewriter keys
who tell no one until they get brave
and crawl off onto the printed page.

I'm getting bored with it,
I tell the typewriter,
this constantly walking around
in wet shoes and then, surprise!
Somehow DECEASED keeps getting
stamped in red over the word HOPE.

And I who keep falling thankfully
into each new pillow of belief,
finding my Mercy Street,
kissing it and tenderly gift-wrapping my love,
am beginning to wonder just what
the planets had in mind on November 9th, 1928.
The pillows are ripped away,
the hand guillotined,
dog shit thrown into the middle of a laugh,
a hornets' nest building into the hi-fi speaker
and leaving me in silence,
where, without music,
I become a cracked orphan.

Well,
one gets out of bed
and the planets don't always hiss
or muck up the day, each day.
As for the pain and its multiplying teaspoon,
perhaps it is a medicine
that will cure the soul
of its greed for love
next Thursday.

DEMON

A young man is afraid of his demon and puts his hand
over the demon's mouth sometimes . . . — D. H. Lawrence

I mentioned my demon to a friend
and the friend swam in oil and came forth to me
greasy and cryptic
and said,
"I'm thinking of taking him out of hock.
I pawned him years ago."
Who would buy?
The pawned demon,
Yellowing with forgetfulness
and hand at his throat?
Take him out of hock, my friend,
but beware of the grief
that will fly into your mouth like a bird.

My demon,
too often undressed,
too often a crucifix I bring forth,
too often a dead daisy I give water to
too often the child I give birth to
and then abort, nameless, nameless . . .
earthless.

Oh demon within,
I am afraid and seldom put my hand up
to my mouth and stitch it up
covering you, smothering you

from the public voyeury eyes
of my typewriter keys.
If I should pawn you,
what bullion would they give for you,
what pennies, swimming in their copper kisses
what bird on its way to perishing?

No.
No.
I accept you,
you come with the dead who people my dreams,
who walk all over my desk
(as in Mother, cancer blossoming on her
Best & Co. tits —
waltzing with her tissue paper ghost)
the dead, who give sweets to the diabetic in me,
who give bolts to the seizure of roses
that sometimes fly in and out of me.
Yes.
Yes.
I accept you, demon.
I will not cover your mouth.
If it be man I love, apple laden and foul
or if it be woman I love, sick unto her blood
and its sugary gasses and tumbling branches.

Demon come forth,
even if it be God I call forth
standing like a carrion,
wanting to eat me,
starting at the lips and tongue.
And me wanting to glide into His spoils,
I take bread and wine,

and the demon farts and giggles,
at my letting God out of my mouth
anonymous woman
at that anonymous altar.

THE SEA CORPSE

The beach was crowded,
people tossed like ripe corn,
buttering themselves as they went
and on the dunes thousands of crabs,
moved their yellowy eyes.
Up above the sea grass
flew like a woman's hair in labor.
And you were at the sea.
Perhaps you did not notice,
that it had gone out,
a permanent removal.
I was at the same sea but in a different locale
and saw only it had gone out like an awful visitor.
There was no suck and slump.
But that's the least of it.
Right out to the horizon
it had been removed surgically;
the blue, the green, the gray, the blood red,
had been sucked out of it
and the water of it, the brine of it
had gone somewhere else.
Not even a tide pool remained.
I think I cried
but perhaps I didn't.
I flew into my head and there
fifty tiny oceans lay in a coffin.
Their coffins were pink and embossed and gaudy

and after the rabbi had sung over them,
they were quickly buried.
I did not cry then.
I knew it was a natural order.
The centuries of our blue mothers came
and we spoke to them, adored their moods,
immersed in their holy waters
but one day they were dead.
And I threw a little earth
on the pink coffin
covered by the fake plastic grass
and said O.K., God,
if it's the end of the world,
it must be necessary.

THERE YOU WERE

There you were,
solitary, 7:00 A.M.
surveying your own unpeopled beach
and the sea, that day,
was as calm as an unplayed piano,
and the gulls popped in and out,
softly, softly and your eyes grew soft
with their unused power
and your defenses swept out into
the baby tongues of the tide,
that day, Barbara,
when an entire house broke out of the sea
and collapsed at your feet.
And you strode toward it
to see if it had a problem,
or if the sea-carpenter in you
could set it upright.

This was pure instinct
and though as you peeked in the ghosty windows,
and felt the nails growing the wrong way out
you had only a small fear
and the fear was not for yourself
but for her, lest she drift outward,
into the sea at war with itself.
You laughed at her doors,

and opened them with care,
lest a convulsion crush the structure.

The house waited on your private beach
each day,
when you had the time to return to her.
And you so often had the time,
even when fury blew out her chimney,
even when love lifted the shingles
even when loss after loss
cracked her cage
and the sea boiled at the edge of the structure.
Yet you battled for that house
with a small delight in your power
over the teeth that had bitten it in two.

The house of my body has spoken
often as you rebuild me like blocks,
and promise to come visit
when I'm finally adjusted on safe land,
and am livable, joist to joist
with storm windows and screens,
mattresses, fixtures,
sand dollars, cups —
inhabitable and all that.
But not for sale!
Perhaps when I'm an antique,
as a gift,
cranky but firm,
I'll take in boarders
who admire my ocean view.

THE CONSECRATING MOTHER

I stand before the sea
and it rolls and rolls in its green blood
saying, "Do not give up one god
for I have a handful."
The trade winds blew
in their twelve-fingered reversal
and I simply stood on the beach
while the ocean made a cross of salt
and hung up its drowned
and they cried *Deo Deo*.
The ocean offered them up in the vein of its might.
I wanted to share this
but I stood alone like a pink scarecrow.
The ocean steamed in and out,
the ocean gasped upon the shore
but I could not define her,
I could not name her mood, her locked-up faces.
Far off she rolled and rolled
like a woman in labor
and I thought of those who had crossed her,
in antiquity, in nautical trade, in slavery, in war.
I wondered how she had borne those bulwarks.
She should be entered skin to skin,
and put on like one's first or last cloth,
entered like kneeling your way into church,
descending into that ascension,
though she be slick as olive oil,

as she climbs each wave like an embezzler of white.
The big deep knows the law as it wears its gray hat,
though the ocean comes in its destiny,
with its one hundred lips,
and in moonlight she comes in *her* nudity,
flashing breasts made of milk-water,
flashing buttocks made of unkillable lust,
and at night when you enter her
you shine like a neon soprano.

I am that clumsy human
on the shore
loving you, coming, coming,
going,
and wish to put my thumb on you
like The Song of Solomon.